Learn About Animals

Bat

By Cecilia Minden

This is a bat.

This bat is small.

This bat is big!

The Sun is up.

This bat rests.

It has a pup.

Its pup rests on it.

It must hunt at dusk.

Bats hunt bugs.

But the Sun is up.

Mom and pup can rest.

Rest up, pup!

Word List

sight words

a
small
The
the
This

short i words

big
is
It
it
Its

short a words

and
at
bat
Bats
can
has

short e words

rest
Rest
rests

short o words

Mom
on

short u words

bugs
But
dusk
hunt
must
pup
Sun
up

49 Words

This is a bat.
This bat is small.
This bat is big!
The Sun is up.
This bat rests.
It has a pup.
Its pup rests on it.
It must hunt at dusk.
Bats hunt bugs.
But the Sun is up.
Mom and pup can rest.
Rest up, pup!

Published in the United States of America by Cherry Lake Publishing Group
Ann Arbor, Michigan
www.cherrylakepublishing.com

Photo Credits: © Joel Sartore/National Geographic Photo Ark, cover; © Passakorn Umpornmaha/Shutterstock, 2; © Corina Daniela Obertas/Shutterstock, 3; © Puffin's Pictures/Shutterstock, 4; © Lucian Coman/Shutterstock, 5, 11; © Robby Holmwood/Shutterstock, 6; © francesco de marco/Shutterstock, 7, 12, 13; © Gert Very/Shutterstock, 8; © Tae PY15MU/Shutterstock, 9; © Young Swee Ming/Shutterstock, 10; © Farinoza/Dreamstime.com, 15; © Joel Sartore/National Geographic Photo Ark, back cover

Cherry Blossom Press is an imprint of Cherry Lake Publishing Group.

Library of Congress Cataloging-in-Publication Data
has been filed and is available at catalog.loc.gov.

Printed in the United States of America

Cecilia Minden is the former director of the Language and Literacy Program at Harvard Graduate School of Education. She earned her PhD in Reading Education at the University of Virginia. Dr. Minden has written extensively for early readers. She is passionate about matching children to the very book they need to improve their skills and progress to a deeper understanding of all the wonder books can hold.

Cherry Blossom Press